Dragon in the jam

Written by Clare Helen Welsh

Illustrated by Sian James

Collins

Star and Dad are at the shops.
Dad points to the list.

They need a beetroot, a bunch of greens and a tin of sweetcorn.

"Can we get crisps?" begs Star.
Dad frowns. "No, crisps are not on
the list."

"Can we get sweets?" begs Star.
Dad groans. "No, sweets are not on
the list."

"Can we get jam?" begs Star.
Dad agrees. "Yes, jam is on the list."

Star gets a fright. There is a bright green dragon in the jar!

slurp

The dragon swoops down and chomps a bun. It glugs some sweet milk!

Star starts a trail. The dragon looks at the trail of food.

Then it sees the bunch of greens.
Chomp! It smells the sweetcorn. Munch!

The dragon slurps the sweetcorn.
Star puts the dragon on the shelf.

At the till, Star's Dad wins a free plush dragon.

You are the winner!

12

Star hugs the bright green dragon.
"Meet my dragon, Slurper!" she grins.

Star's plan

🐾 Review: After reading 🐾

Use your assessment from hearing the children read to choose any GPCs, words or tricky words that need additional practice.

Read 1: Decoding

- Focus on words with adjacent consonants and long vowels.
    - Point to **points** on page 2. Ask the children to sound out and blend. (*p/oi/n/t/s*)
    - Ask the children to sound out and blend these words:

        fright   agrees   swoops   Slurper

Read 2: Prosody

- Model reading each page with expression to the children.
- After you have read each page, ask the children to have a go at reading with expression.
- Read the book together with you as the narrator and half the children reading the spoken words for Dad and the other half reading the spoken words for Star.

Read 3: Comprehension

- Turn to pages 14 and 15 and ask the children to retell the story about Star's plan, the trail and what she hoped to do.
- For every question ask the children how they know the answer. Ask:
    - On page 5, why do you think Dad groans? (e.g. *because Star keeps asking for things that aren't on the list*)
    - What frightened Star? (*She sees a bright green dragon in a jar of jam.*)
    - Why does Star lay a trail of food? (e.g. *so the dragon follows her*)
    - On page 12, what do you think Star is doing? (*looking for the dragon*)
    - On page 13, which dragon is called Slurper? Why is it a good name? (*It is the real dragon. It slurps up milk and food.*)
    - Why does Star give the toy dragon back to the shop assistant? (*because she has her own real dragon!*)